Mariana Plays Pretend

by

Leisa Pasquariello and Jackie Murphy

Marianna Plays Pretend
Art ©2025 Leisa Pasquariello
Words ©2025 Jackie Murphy
Layout and editing ©2025 C. Pelton

This book may not be reused in anyway, with the exception of small excerpts for the purposes of review.

Small Town Press First Printing ©2025

ISBN: 979-8-3492-8781-7

Hello friends! Marianna is my name.

Want to join me on a pretend adventure where I get to be who I dream of becoming one day?

My dream is to someday be the most famous ballerina in the world. In my dream, I twirl gracefully on my toes while receiving applause and flowers from the audience, urging me to continue dancing.

Some days, I dream of being a teacher, instructing children in their ABCs, 123s, and singing fun songs. I would lead the kids outside for some fun on the swings and slides. Having me as your teacher would be really fun.

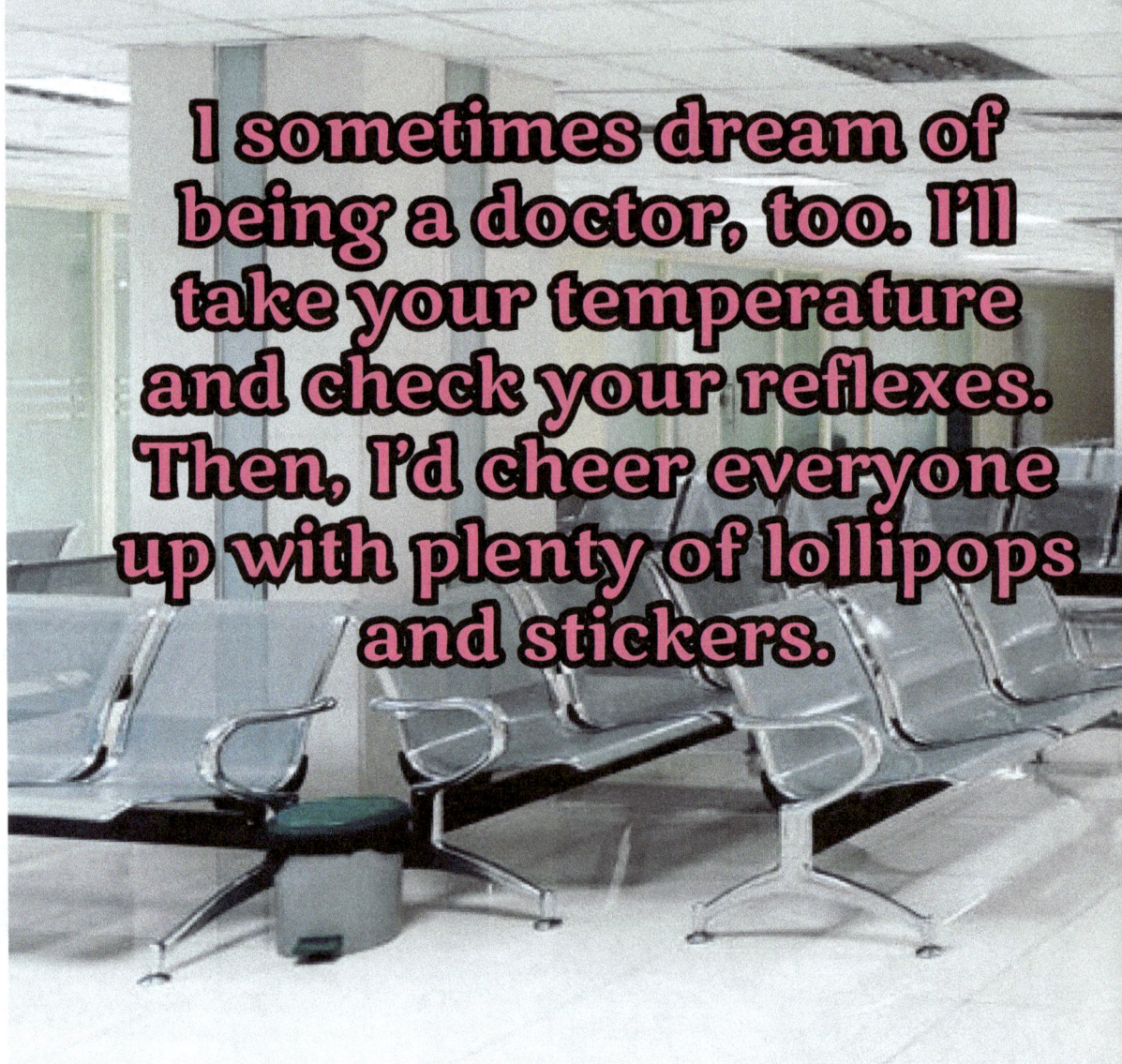

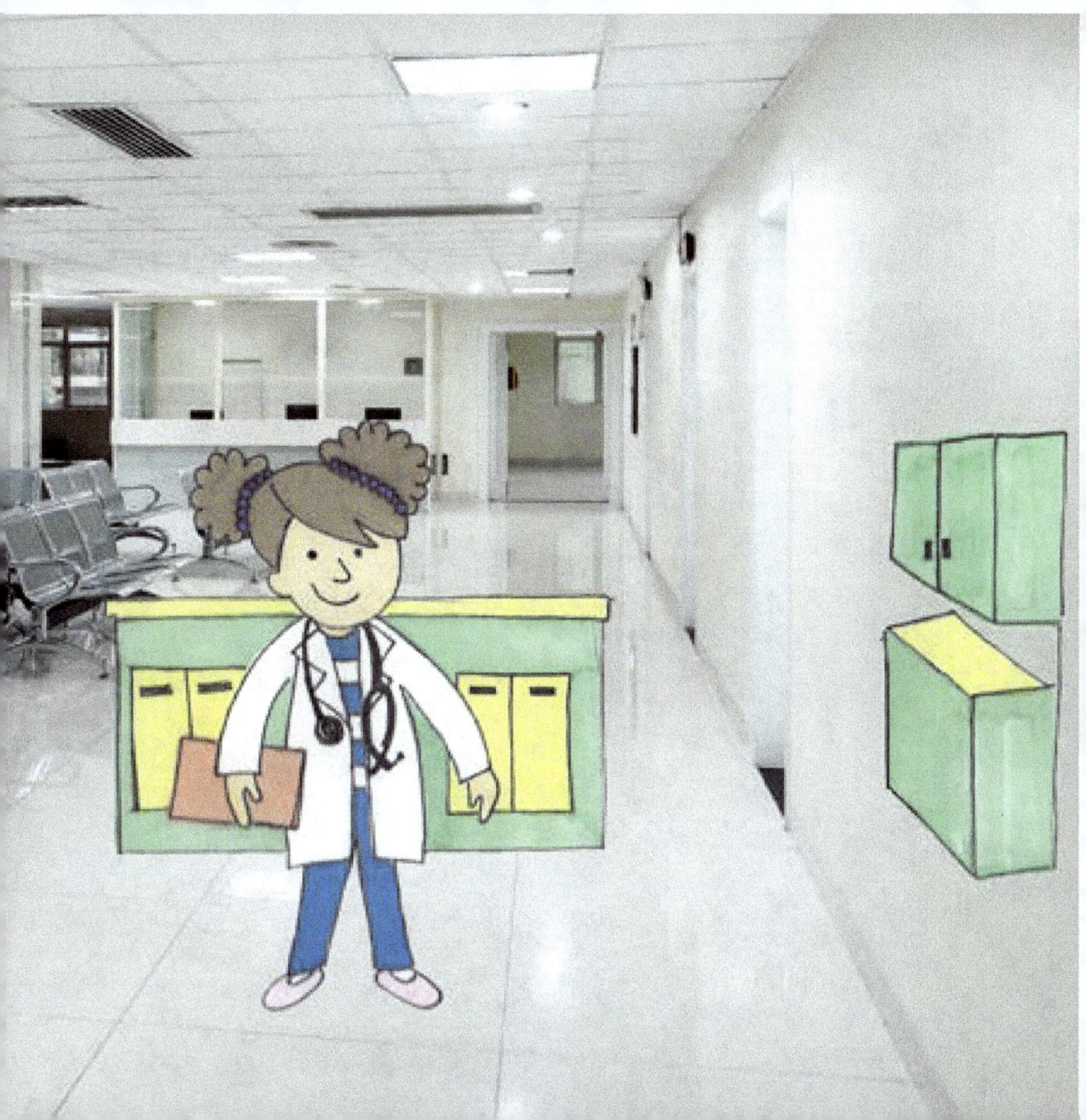

I sometimes dream of becoming a baker. My cooking would include wonderful cakes and many tasty dishes. People from all around the world would come and eat at my restaurant.

Then I dream of becoming the world's most famous artist. I would paint trees, flowers, fruit and butterflies. Homes everywhere would feature my art.

What do you pretend and dream about being?

Are you dreaming of becoming a doctor, teacher, artist, or builder?

With your imagination, you can be anything!!!

www.ingramcontent.com/pod-product-compliance
Lightning Source LLC
LaVergne TN
LVHW081456060526
838201LV00051BA/1817